MW01595287

MAKING YOUR HOME THE GREEN ZONE

PASTORS JOHN AND EVELYN OGLETREE

CROSSBOOKS
PUBLISHING

CrossBooks™
1663 Liberty Drive
Bloomington, IN 47403
www.crossbooks.com
Phone: 1-866-879-0502

First published by CrossBooks 11/3/2009

ISBN: 978-1-6150-7006-0 (sc)

Library of Congress Control Number: 2009939041

Printed in the United States of America
Bloomington, Indiana

This book is printed on acid-free paper.

DEDICATION

We would like to dedicate this book to our mothers, Marion M. Deckard, (80 years of age) and Lela M. Wilson (deceased) who made sure we were raised in godly, healthy and happy homes. We also dedicate this book to our four children Johnny, (35) Lambreni, (33) Joseph (26) and Jordan (22). It is our prayer that they pass this spiritual legacy to their families and generations to come.

ACKNOWLEDGEMENT

We are grateful to the First Metropolitan Church family for allowing us to teach and model family life before them for 23 years. We have raised our children as we led our congregation, and have now established a church that seeks to encourage, empower and equip families. We are so blessed to have a very talented and hard working Administrative Assistant in Paulette Snowden who assists us in the preparation of workshops, seminars, and publications.

INTRODUCTION

IN CENTRAL BAGHDAD THERE IS A four square mile area known as the Green Zone. Its official name originating under the Iraqi Interim Government is the International Zone. Outside of the Green Zone is the contrasting Red Zone. The Red Zone is the unsecured area. But the Green Zone is completely surrounded by high concrete walls, T-Walls (reinforced and blast-proof concrete slabs), and barbed wire. Access is available only through a handful of entry points controlled by Coalition troops.

Time Magazine reports there is a place called Baghdad Country Club, a white cinder-block house with blue trim on a residential street in the Green Zone, where over 800 cold beers might be served to diplomats, security guards and construction workers who frequent it. The Green Zone makes the city, where buildings have been bombed, cars burned and blown up, look serene. It is protected on two sides by the caramel colored waters of the Tigris and is the home to thousands of people, including many members of the Iraqi government. It is the seat of U. S. power. The Al-Rasheed Hotel offers rooms at $280-a-night. A clerk there is quoted as saying: *"Living here is like living in Europe. You miss nothing, starting with electricity, power, water and security. Outside the gates is hell."*

The Green Zone is lush and tropical with very little humidity. Private villas nestle in the shade of palm trees. It is a Middle Eastern paradise filled with gardens and ponds. Footpaths cross ornamental bridges over streams. There is so much open space in the Green Zone that several groups can live with very little interaction.

Wide boulevards line the area. This is the former preserve of Saddam Hussein and his favorite associates. An area of villas, palaces, and monuments in a park-like setting are visible as far as the eye can see.

The Green Zone is the hub of the vision for the New Iraq. It is almost self-sufficient. It is protected by coils of razor wire, chain-link fences, and armed checkpoints. M1 Abrams tanks, Bradley fighting vehicles and HUMVEES with .50 caliber machine guns on top, guard the Green Zone.

The Green Zone was designed to be an oasis from the chaos outside of it. In the same vein, our homes should be designed to be an oasis from all the trouble in the world that reign outside of it.

CHAPTER ONE

LIVING IN THE GREEN ZONE

OUR HOMES SHOULD BE LIKE THE Green Zone in Baghdad, a place that is serene, satisfying and safe. We should be saying: "Living here is like living in heaven. You miss nothing: food, water, clothing, or security. Outside the walls of our home may be hell, but inside is heaven!"

Outside of our homes is: backstabbing, the rat race, a dog-eat-dog philosophy, bigotry, hatred, jealousy, envy, plots, schemes, mugging, thugs, fraud, deceit, arguments, bitterness, condescension, gossip, betrayal, pink-slips, hoochies, freaks, whores, whore-mongers, drunks, closed doors, crime, abuse, murder, assaults, potholes, profanity, traffic, pedophiles, etc. In other words, it is supposed to be hell "outside" but not inside our home.

When you think about the word 'green' you think about life, newness, freshness, growth, health, productivity, and prosperity. Do these words come to your mind when you think of your home?

God put the first family in a Green Zone in the Garden of Eden. It was His intent for the family to be a place of life, newness, freshness, growth, health, productivity, and prosperity. Consider Genesis 1:27-30: "So God created man in his own image, in the image he created him; male and female he created them. God blessed them and said to them, Be fruitful and increase in number, fill the earth and subdue it. Rule over the fish of the sea and the birds of the air and over every living creature that moves on the ground. Then God said, I give you every seed-bearing plant on the face of the whole earth and every tree that has fruit with seed in it. They will be yours for food. And to all the beasts of the earth and all the birds of the air and all the creatures that move on the ground – everything that has the breath of life in it – I give every green plant for food. And it was so."

Pastor O and Lady O with his mother and their granddaughters
Elianah and Reya

God blessed Adam and Eve, endowing them with the ability, the capacity to reproduce, be fruitful and succeed. This family was to conquer, rule, dominate or bring under their control everything for their advantage in the Garden. It was the first Gated Community. God protected them from all evil and from enemies. It was a place of serenity, satisfaction and safety. Adam and Eve were to have no worries and no fear.

Job knew something about a Green Zone. He was blameless and upright. He had a wife, seven sons and three daughters. He also had a number of servants. He owned seven thousand sheep, three thousand camels, five hundred yoke of oxen and five hundred donkeys. When Satan came before God wanting to mess with Job, God offered Job. But Satan recognized God's protection around Job. "Have you not put a hedge around him and his household and everything he has?" -Job 1:10

A hedge is a restraint, a fence, a wall of safety for the inhabitants and is designed to obstruct certain behavior. The hedge that God puts around a home is like living in the ultimate gated community. It is living in the Green Zone.

When we look at Paul's letter to the Colossians, we believe that this same theme of serenity, satisfaction and safety is strongly suggested. "Wives, submit to your husbands, as is fitting in the Lord. Husbands, love your wives and do not be harsh with them. Children, obey your parents in everything, for this pleases the Lord. Fathers, do not embitter your children, or they will become discouraged." -Colossians 3:18-21

The greatest dysfunction in our homes is spiritual. That's why we must look to the Scriptures to see what God says about the home.

These verses along with Ephesians 5:22-33 have brought much controversy, especially in our postmodern age. We have wives, those expecting to be wives, and even those who don't want to be wives who argue that Paul's instruction is old fashioned, archaic, outdated or uninspired by the Spirit. This issue has become a battleground in contemporary life. Many raise the point that Paul was a man writing from a man's point of view. Therefore, the question arises: Is 'submission" chauvinistic or Christo-centric?

The word 'submission' means to subject oneself, to accept authority, or to be under the authority of. It carries the idea of being submissive willingly, not reluctantly or being compelled. According to the Scripture, a woman should not be made to submit. She is to do it with a willing heart. This means she willingly makes the choice to subject her will, her desires, her opinions to the man that she has chosen to be with in a lifelong covenant relationship.

This is Christo-centric not chauvinistic. That is why Paul uses this phase: As is fitting in the Lord.

This submission does not mean inferiority or insignificance. It does not allow the husband to be a tyrant, a dictator, a macho man, a fool, a drill sergeant, a slave driver or an animal. A wife is not obligated to follow leadership that is unbiblical or demonic. That is like living in hell.

Paul teaches mutual submission. It is not a one-way street. It goes both ways. It fact, the obligation on the man is greater. Husbands are given instruction to be submissive through love. This love is not romantic, passionate, physical or affectionate in nature. The love that Paul instructs for husbands is a selfless and sacrificial demonstration.

The word for love means: the God kind of love. It is the highest form of Christian love. It carries the idea of showing love or taking pleasure in a selfless, sacrificial demonstration. It is the love a man chooses because of his covenant in spite of the circumstances.

The husband is to be the spiritual head of the family and the wife is to acknowledge his leadership. Husbands should remember that if they are the head, the wife is the neck. The neck supports the head. There is mutual dependence. The kind of head Paul is talking about is explained in Ephesians 5:23, 25, and 28. "For the husband is the head of the wife as Christ is the head of the church, his body, of which he is the Savior...

"Husbands, love your wives, just as Christ loves the church and gave himself for her...

"In the same way, husbands ought to love their wives as their own bodies. He who loves his wife loves himself."

Husbands are to follow the model of Christ by loving their wives. Her submission to him is the result of the love that he demonstrates. His headship must be loving, caring, sacrificial, giving, compassionate and understanding. Like Jesus. Being head should not be a power struggle. Jesus did not throw His weight around or go about always announcing who He was and what His position was.

Paul also tells husbands "not to be harsh with them." This meant not to be embittered with their wives or not to make them bitter. In Roman culture, the husband had absolute authority and women were seen as property.

Even in America decades ago, women did not work, were not educated, could not vote, and could not preach. The idea of submission meant total, unquestioned submission. This was not God's original plan. We are in a new day. Myles Monroe spoke of this at the For Men's Only Conference sponsored by Bishop T. D. Jakes. But now, women work, and are as educated, if not more educated than men, own property, have money and cannot fit into a BC, AD, 18th, 19th, or 20th century philosophy.

Paul teaches against this type of philosophy. The love he speaks about is not demanding, derogatory, demonic, demeaning, disturbing, disappointing or displeasing. Without Christ-like love from husbands, the home will be like living in hell. Husbands must have the right attitude about their wives. Proverbs 18:22 encourages a right attitude when it says: "He who finds a wife finds what is good and receives favor from the Lord."

Through many years of counseling couples, we have developed a top ten list of why there is fire or hell in homes. The following list is not gender based.

- Not living by biblical principles
- No order in the home
- Refusal to support the family financially
- Explosive personality
- Abusive behavior
- Lack of respect
- Too much debt
- Infidelity
- Spiritual hypocrisy
- Sexual manipulation

We have also found that when a wife submits in the Lord to a husband who is a Christ following, loving leader, the home will be a place of serenity, satisfaction and safety. And, when the husband and wife get their act together, children can be properly raised and held accountable.

Paul has instructions for children also. Children are to obey their parents in everything for this "pleases the Lord." It is the parent who has the responsibility of guiding the child toward God and maturity. In the Old Testament a disobedient child was severely punished.

> "Anyone who attacks his father or his
> mother must be put to death." -Exodus 21:15

> "If anyone curses his father or mother,
> he must be put to death. He has cursed
> his father or his mother, and his blood
> will be on his own head." -Leviticus 20:9

A child's command to be obedient is balanced by the command to the fathers "not to embitter" their children. The interpretation means not to provoke, irritate or exasperate children. Parents are charged in Proverbs 22:6 to:

> "Train a child in a way he should go,
> and when he is old he will not turn
> from it."

Training is hard work. It is 24/7 from birth to 21 years. Spiritual dysfunction exists when the responsibility of training the child is placed on the world, the school or the criminal justice system. When a baby is born parents are obligated by God to nurture, train and see that the child develops according to God's plans; according to the child's gifts, personality, and intellect.

Parents must be careful in exercising their authority. They should not nag, be overly critical, belittle, show favoritism, fail to encourage or show affection, or set unrealistic goals or abandon their children emotionally or physically.

> Brothers, Sisters, Children!
> It's time to live in the Green Zone!
> The Green Zone is serene, satisfying and safe. The Green Zone glorifies God. You find these attributes in a Green Zone home:
> - Godliness – piety, devotion and worship.
>   Lives that are pleasing to God.
>
> - Grace – the inexhaustible quality to
>   forgive and to bless.
>
> - Gentleness – a disposition of humility,
>   courteousness and unpretentiousness.
>
> - Goodness – benevolence, compassion,
>   empathy, mercy, patience.
>
> - Give and take – not having to have your
>   way, prioritizing the interest of the other.

If we do these things our home will be homes of life, freshness, growth, newness, health, productivity and prosperity. One of the popular TV shows today is "Extreme Makeover – Home Edition." It is a show where a team takes an old, dirty, worn down, run-down, unsanitary, dilapidated home, remodels it and makes it valuable and livable again.

Your home might need an Extreme Makeover today. Here is what they do on the show. This is also what you need to do to undergo an Extreme Spiritual Makeover of your home.

- Assess the state of the house
- Tear down what is rotten, weak, unnecessary or unlivable
- Haul it away
- Start the remodeling process
- Add to, change, fix, rearrange, brighten, open up, fortify
- Present the new to God and then to the world

Decide today to make your home the Green Zone.
    It's time to live in the Green Zone.
    It's time to live in the abundant life.
    It's time to live in the newness of Christ.
    It's time to live in freedom.
    It's time to live in spiritual growth.
    It's time to live in health.
    It's time to live in productivity.
    It's time to live in prosperity.

It is time for your home to be a place of serenity, satisfaction and safety. All dangers, darkness, deception, destruction, decay, delusions, degeneration, demons, deterioration, degradation and dehumanization should be kept on the outside of our homes, and not ever allowed on the inside of our home.

Pastor O performs Ordination for son Joseph.

NOTES

A godly home can be seen in the eyes of its children.

The outside of a home does not always reflect what's going on inside the home.

CHAPTER TWO

IS HOME SAFE ANYMORE?

EVEN IN THE SUCCESSFUL DEVELOPMENT OF the Green Zone, American forces and the Iraqi Interim Government are realizing the tenaciousness of the enemy. The headlines from Baghdad read like this lately.

Baghdad's Green Zone Rocked By Explosions!

For the first time since the war began terrorists have been able to penetrate the Green Zone. The Green Zone was once the United States' impenetrable fortress in Iraq. But now there is terror in the heart of the American presence. There is now explosions and smoke coming from the Green Zone. Now hell is inside and violence is inside. Fear is inside. And death is inside.

You may identify with this as it relates to your home. Either, you have been there or you are there now. It could be that at one time you thought your home was a Green Zone.

- At one time there was serenity, satisfaction and safety there.
- At one time there was joy and laughter.
- At one time there was harmony.
- At one time there was communication.
- At one time there was romance.
- At one time there was dreaming instead of scheming.

- At one time the bills were getting paid.
- At one time there was family prayer.
- At one time there were dreams for the future.

But now with all the adversity your family is facing, you wonder: "Is our home safe anymore?"

What was once safe is now unsafe. Has your home been rocked with explosions? Is smoke coming from your home? Is hell inside? Is violence inside? Is fear inside? Is death inside? Are dreams being killed? Is hope being killed? Is joy being killed?

What happened? What happened to your wall, your fortification, and your security? You need to know that there will always be an attack on the Green Zone. The adversary cannot stand you living in the Green Zone.

Genesis helps us understand this with a portrait of the first family, Adam and Eve. They were in their Green Zone. Everything was peaches and cream in the Garden of Eden. They had everything. They did not want for anything. Then the insurgency came.

The crafty serpent showed up to wreck things. He asked: "Did God really say, 'You must not eat from any tree in the garden?'

Eve answered: "We may eat fruit from the trees in the garden, but God did say, 'You must not eat fruit from the tree that is in the middle of the garden, and you must not touch it, or you will die.'

The serpent came back: 'You will not surely die. For God knows that when you eat of it your eyes will be opened, and you will be like God, knowing good and evil.'

The Bible says when Eve looked at the fruit and saw that it was good to eat and pleasing to the eye and desirable for wisdom, she took it and ate. Then she gave Adam some of the fruit and he ate also. Then the eyes of both of them were opened and they realized they were naked.

After God spoke to them and pronounced judgment on them, we find this in verses 23 and 24: "So the Lord God banished him from the Garden of Eden to work the ground from which he had been taken. After he drove the man out, he placed on the east side of the Garden of Eden cherubim and a flaming sword flashing back and forth to guard the way to the tree of life."

What happened to Adam and Eve? They opened the door for the enemy: the ear gate, the eye gate and the mouth gate. They experienced an attack on their home. The very first insurgency on earth was against the family.

An insurgent is a rebel against a lawful government. In the Garden of Eden God had established His kingdom through Adam and Even and the insurgent who had been thrown out of heaven came against God's rule on earth. The first attack by the devil on earth was against the family. And the devil is still messing up families.

- The devil is still showing up where there is peace and happiness.
- The devil is still deceptively questioning God's Word.
- The devil is still calling God a liar.
- The devil is still misleading God's children.

We used to say: "The devil is busy." Well, he is busy in our homes! Have you seen him lately? Is your home safe anymore?

Any arguments lately? Any bitterness lately? Any thoughts of divorce lately? Any fowl language lately? Any plotting and scheming lately? And disfavor with God lately? The devil has been busy!

It was the chief insurgent that attacked Job's home. He messed up his happy home. He had been roaming the earth going back and forth and saw the blameless, upright Job as a prime target for terrorism. The five hundred oxen and donkeys were attacked and stolen. The seven thousand sheep were burnt up. The tree thousand camels were raided and carried off. Then his seven sons and three daughters were killed.

Peter writes of the chief insurgent: "Your enemy the devil prowls around like a roaring lion looking for someone to devour."

-1 Peter 5:8

The devil is after your home, if your home is in a Green Zone!

It is important to note that your home is being attacked on the inside by forces initiated from the outside. Someone who has access someone who could get through the security clearance, and set off explosions in the Green Zone. The attacks may have come from some unsuspecting person who you believed had a right to be inside.

The chief insurgent, the enemy, is so crafty that he disguises himself so that he can enter undetected. He is in disguise. In Baghdad, one of the bombers inside the Green Zone was believed to be a bodyguard for a lawmaker. That is the nature of the enemy. Like the serpent in the Garden of Eden, who would have thought he was the enemy? There were other animals and living creatures there and God had seen that it was good. God warned about a tree, not a serpent. "And no wonder, for Satan himself masquerades as an angel of light. It is not surprising then, if his servants masquerade as servants of righteousness." -2 Corinthians 11:14, 15

The person on the inside causing death and destruction in the home may be you. The comedian Flip Wilson used to say: "The devil made me do it." You must realize that the devil can only influence you. He cannot and has not made you do anything.

Can it be that he has influenced you to be the insurgent in your own home? The insurgent's methods for destruction are hidden. Are you in disguise? Are you wearing a mask? Are you hiding anything that could potentially be explosive? Are you hiding any true emotions or feelings, relationships, sins, debt, money, accounts, gifts, plans, dreams, books, magazines, websites, pain, sickness, changes, places you frequent? The old TV game show had this title that is appropriate to people in our homes: I've Got A Secret.

The enemy majors on negatively influencing people inside your home. It could be your friend, co-worker, neighbor or relative that the enemy uses to influence you against your own home. Or, someone single may be dating someone who has something hidden. And the person is hiding something that can destroy you. You won't find out what he or she is hiding until you get married.

One of the tactics the enemy uses is the one he used in the Garden of Eden. He questions what God has said through someone who has your attention.

He questions what God speaks in Colossians 3:18-21 "Wives, submit to your husbands, as is fitting in the Lord. Husbands, love your wives and do not be harsh with them. Children, obey your parents in everything, for this pleases the Lord. Fathers, do not embitter your children, or they will become discouraged."

The enemy questions what God said in 1 Peter 3:1-7. "Wives, in the same way be submissive to your husbands, so that, if any of them do not believe the word they may be won over without words by the behavior of their wives. Your beauty should not come from outward adornment, such as braided hair and the wearing of gold jewelry and fine clothes. Instead, it should be that of your inner self, the unfading beauty of a gentle and quiet spirit, which is of great worth in God's sight. Husbands, in the same way be considerate as you live with your wives, and treat them with respect as the weaker partner and as heirs with you of the gracious gift of life, so that nothing will hinder your prayers."

The enemy questions what God said in Luke 12:22, 31. "Then Jesus said to his disciples: Therefore I tell you, do not worry about your life, what you will eat; or about your body, what you will wear… But seek His kingdom, and these things will be given to you as well."

The enemy questions what Jesus said in Matthew 19:4-6. "Haven't you read…that at the beginning the Creator made them male and female, and said, For this reason a man will leave his father and mother and be united to his wife, and the two will become one flesh. So they are no longer two, but one. Therefore what God has joined together, let man not separate."

The enemy questions what the Word of God says in

1 Corinthians 13:4-7. "Love is patient, love is kind. It does not envy, it does not boast, it is not proud. It is not easily angered, it keeps no record of wrongs. Love does not delight in evil but rejoices with the truth. It always protects, always trusts, always hopes, always perseveres."

The enemy questions what God said in 1 Corinthians 7:4. "The wife's body does not belong to her alone but also to her husband. In the same way, the husband's body does not belong to him alone but also to his wife."

The enemy questions what God said in 1 Corinthians 7:8,9. "Now to the unmarried and the widows I say: It is good for them to stay unmarried, as I am. But if they cannot control themselves, they should marry, for it is better to marry than to burn with passion."

After the devil questions you deceptively, he then calls God a liar. When you listen to and obey Satan, you call God a liar. He makes you think that God is trying to hold back something from you or that God doesn't want you to be happy or blessed. He messes with your mind to make *you the insurgent in your own home*. He makes you rebel against God. When you rebel against God, you bring in the explosives that will damage your own home.

Is your home safe? Have you made it unsafe?

When the home is hit with explosives, hell has come inside. You need to know:

- The hidden is hostile to your home.
- The hidden will hinder growth and life.
- The hidden will hold you hostage to your sin.
- The hidden will hand your family over to Satan.
- The hidden will make it hard to sleep at night.

- The hidden will bring harshness and hatred.
- The hidden will make your heart hard against God.
- The hidden will hold up your next level blessing.

Ask yourself, did I bring these explosives into my home? Did I allow them to come in?

> What are you to do? Peter helps us in 1 Peter 5:9-10.
> "Be self-controlled and alert... Resist him,
> standing firm in the faith, because you
> know that your brothers are undergoing
> the same kind of sufferings."

The first thing we need to do in our homes is keep our heads clear so that we can be alert. We need to stay awake when it comes to the enemy. After the wedding, the new cars, the new house or apartment, the new furniture, the clothes, the jewelry, the jobs, the restaurants, the movies and the credit cards, it is easy to not be alert. Remember, the enemy has a special weapon for each of us with our name on it. There is a weapon with your family's name on it. The enemy knows your address.

When you are alert:
- You will be aware that there is an enemy.
- You will be conscious of anything that looks suspicious.
- You will be able to identify his tactics.

When you are alert:
- You won't listen to the enemy.
- You won't talk back to the enemy.
- You will destroy the enemy the first time he speaks.

Eve was not alert. Adam was not alert. Eve had no business talking to the serpent. Adam and Eve did not realize that the serpent had no authority in the Garden of Eden. He did not create the garden. He did not place them in the garden. He did not give them rule over it. God did! The enemy did not save you, give you your spouse, give you your children, give you your job or business, nor did he give you your home. So do not listen to him. Don't talk to him. Keep your eye gates and your ear gates on the Word of God, which is the gateway to a safe home.

You have to be alert to what the enemy is putting in your spirit. You have to be alert to what the enemy is putting in your mind. You have to be alert to a voice that is contrary to God's voice. You have to be alert to what the enemy is trying to do to your family. You have to be alert to God's truth for you and your family.

Then you have to resist the enemy. The word 'resist' means to oppose. You have to oppose the devil. You cannot allow him to use you. You cannot allow him to put a mask on you. He is your opponent, not your friend. He is a deceiver. He is your adversary. Resist him or he will kill, steal and destroy your family.

You have to oppose his tactics, his questioning of God, his calling your God a liar, his playing with your mind. Resist him. Oppose him by standing firm in the faith. You have to take a stand with the word. You cannot lie down and quit or surrender. You have to take a stand. You have to be steadfast, unmovable, always abounding in the work of the Lord.

Even if you have messed up and allowed yourself to be used, even though the explosions are going off in your home, even if there is fear and terror in your home, you can stop it now by taking a stand in the faith. Find a scripture. Go to your prayer closet. Turn the television to Christian stations. Play Gospel music. Plead the blood over your home. Play one of the pastor's messages in your car or home. Whatever you do resist the enemy by standing firm in the faith. Cover your gates with God's words.

The next thing you need to do is realize that your family is not the only one being attacked. The enemy likes to isolate you and make you think that you and your family are the ones being attacked. But Peter lets us know that believers and their families all over the world are experiencing the same type of suffering.

There is good news in this text for your family. Peter writes further:

> "And the God of all grace, who called
> you to his eternal glory in Christ,
> after you have suffered awhile, will
> himself restore you and make you strong,
> firm and steadfast. To him be the power
> forever and ever. Amen."

Peter tells us that there is grace available for our homes. He tells us that after we have suffered awhile, meaning after we have been terrorized, after the fear, the worry, the pain, the bitterness, God will bring restoration. God will make things right again. Your home will be safe again. There will be serenity and satisfaction again.

God is in the Restoration Business! If you stop listening to and talking to Satan and start listening to and talking to God, God will restore:

- Your job
- Your peace
- Your love
- Your prosperity
- Your dreams
- Your intimacy

Peter says not only will God restore you, but He will make you strong, firm and steadfast.

A Family that Plays Together will Stay Together!

Pastor O with granddaughter Reya.

Pastor and Lady O dance with daughter, Lambreni and granddaughter Reya.

(L-R) Lady O and her girls: Sherrell, Lady O, Quinita, and Lambreni.

NOTES

NOTES

CHAPTER THREE
CHECKPOINTS FOR THE HOME

LARRY DIAMOND, A FORMER ADVISOR TO the United States in Baghdad, was asked how the terrorists have been able to successfully penetrate the Green Zone. He stated:

> "Well obviously it's a failure of security
> if the purpose of all these checkpoints and
> sandbags, and reviews and so on, is to keep
> the zone secure and they got in and killed
> people anyway – then yes, security failed
> in some way."

Time Magazine reports that the Green Zone is guarded by a "crazy quilt of security personnel." U. S. soldiers do not only staff this "quilt", but also the Iraqi army, Iraqi police and other approved soldiers and guards. Once security has been breached, the checkpoints become the center of the investigation.

A checkpoint is a place where something is halted for inspection. It is a place where vehicles or pedestrians are stopped in order to enforce the law or to enforce security measures.

You, no doubt, are familiar with a checkpoint if you have traveled by plane, especially since "nine eleven." The terrorists were able to do the damage they did because they got through the checkpoints at various airports.

(L-R - front) Elianah, Adaiah; (L-R middle) Jordan, Pastor O, Sherrell, Jaiden, Joseph, Pastor Evelyn, Lambreni Waddell, Mary Martin; (Back) Avery Waddell

Your home needs a checkpoint for its peace and security. If there is going to be serenity, satisfaction and safety in your home, you have to pay close attention to your home's checkpoint.

In his fourth chapter, James is writing about conflict experienced within a congregation, in other words, a church fight. He addresses the subject of personal relationships that have gone sour among people who were to be known by their love for each other.

"By this all men will know that you are my disciples, if you love one another." -John 13:35

The conflict that James writes about is not between believer and non-believer. It was between believers. This passage of Scripture can appropriately be applied to our homes. James asks: What causes fights and quarrels among you?

Another way of asking is: What causes all the hell in the church? And, when we look at the family, we could ask: What causes all the hell in our homes? James answers his own inquiry: Don't they come from your desires that battle within you?

James gives people in conflict a checkpoint for serenity, satisfaction and safety. The breach in the church's security, as well as in the home, is at the checkpoint, the place where inspections are supposed to take place to ensure security.

What James describes in the church is also happening in our homes. In verse 1, he uses the word "fights", which refers to a state of war or armed conflict. And he uses the word "quarrels", which refers to disputes, strife, skirmishes, or specific battles. He paints the scene of a war zone where there is a struggle between powers with intense indignation.

- Sides have been chosen
- Positions have been dug in
- Weapons have been loaded and pointed
- The objective is to win at all cost

Does this sound like what is going on in your home?

What is sad about this is that our children, relatives, and friends get caught in the crossfire of arguments, power struggles, the blaming, the verbal putdowns, the bypassing of authority, the silent treatment, the neglecting of each other, the holding back of love and affection when hell is in our homes.

According to James, it is all due to one source – one's inward desires, cravings or pleasures. The Greek word used here is *hedone* from which we derive the English word *hedonism*. The philosophy of hedonism is that pleasure is the main goal in life. Hedonists are lovers of self, lovers of money, boastful, arrogant, revilers, disobedient to authority, ungrateful, unholy, unloving, malicious gossips, irreconcilable, brutal, treacherous, reckless, conceited and lovers of pleasure, rather than lovers of God (2 Timothy 3:2-4).

Outward conflict is always a result of one's inner conflict. Paul describes the inner conflict in Romans 7:21-25. "So I find this law at work: When I want to do good, evil is right there with me. For in my inner being I delight in God's law; but I see another law at work in the members of my body waging war against the law of my mind and making me a prisoner of the law of sin at work within my members. What a wretched man I am! Who will rescue me from this body of death? Thanks be to God – through Jesus Christ our Lord."

The flesh is always craving, yearning, pulling, urging and grasping for pleasure against God's word. When this happens, you want what you want. You want it how you want it, when you want it, and where you want it. And, you want it now! This creates an inner battle because these desires, lusts, or pleasures become difficult to control.

Paul writes: "You want something but don't get it. You kill and covet, but you cannot have what you want. You quarrel and fight."

A wife or a husband with a frustrated desire is a walking bomb that if not defused will one day explode. That is why you need a checkpoint. In Baghdad before people enter the Green Zone they have to be sniffed by dogs, go through medal detectors, be body scanned and patted down many times.

As we live together in our homes, we need to go through a checkpoint to see if we are carrying destructive explosives. We need to go through a spiritual search, a spiritual sniffing, a spiritual demon detector, a spiritual scan and a spiritual pat down. Our frustrated desires need to be checked because James says if not, they lead to quarrelling, fighting, murder and covetousness. Desires for one's own pleasure threaten serenity, satisfaction and safety.

It could be desires for:

- Food and more food
- Drink and more drink
- Drugs and more drugs

- Sex and more sex
- Possessions and more possessions
- Money and more money
- Property and more property
- Recognition and more recognition
- Power and more power
- Vengeance and more vengeance

All these desires can get out of control and bring explosions when one does not get what one wants. When desires get out of control, God gets no glory. That is why you need to go through the checkpoint:

- Before you enter your home
- Before you say what is on your mind
- Before you withdraw and get cold
- Before you spend some money
- Before you call your mama or a friend
- Before you snap at your children

And, if you are single, you need a checkpoint to see if you are a walking bomb ready to explode because of your fleshly baggage, your selfish ways, your hurt, your materialism, your compulsive spending, your low self-esteem, etc.

And, you need the checkpoint for the man or woman you are interested in or dating to see if there are some potential explosions waiting because of his or her fleshly habits, baggage, sedition, perversions, narcissism, witchcraft, jealousy, envy, wickedness, etc.

James recognizes that people in conflict need prayer. On one hand, there are those who get so caught up in the struggle that they do not pray. "You do not have, because you do not ask God."

In many instances, the war could be over and the battle won if those fighting would take time to pray. Have you prayed about your situation? When believing people in conflict do not pray, usually it is because:

- They have already taken matters in their own hands using their own wisdom and power.
- They did not believe God would or could solve the conflict.
- They are concerned God does not agree with their position.

When people are in conflict, they need to go through a checkpoint to see if they are lacking when it comes to prayer. James mentions that there are some people praying but they get the same results of those not praying. "When you ask, you do not receive, because you ask with wrong motives, that you may spend what you get on your pleasures."

These types of prayers talk to God but with the wrong motivation. They are not concerned with right or God's will. Their aim in prayer is to manipulate God to act on their behalf for their own selfish reasons. They act like God can't read their minds.

James says these people only pray to satisfy their lusts. The Greek word James uses for "ask" means to plead or beg. Understand this truth: begging God will get you nowhere if you have the wrong motive. When you are in conflict, you need to go through the prayer checkpoint to determine if:

- Your desire is to get revenge.
- Your desire is to make you look good even if you are wrong.
- Your desire is to win at all cost.
- Your receiving from God will only foster pride. (You get the glory, not God.)

Prayer does not guarantee a yes from God. But when you pray right, look for God to answer. When you go through the checkpoint, you pray right: "Do not be anxious about anything, but in everything by prayer and petition, with thanksgiving, present your request to God.

And the peace that transcends all understanding, will guard your hearts and your minds in Christ Jesus." -Philippians 4:6,7

"This is the confidence we have in approaching God: that if we ask anything according to his will, he hears us. And if we know that he hears us – whatever we ask – we know that we have what we asked of him." -1 John 5:14,15

Go through the checkpoint so that you will say 'Not my will but they will be done.'

James uses a marriage term to describe the sin of the people in conflict. They are called adulterous people, a term meaning spiritual unfaithfulness. "But like a woman unfaithful to her husband, so you have been unfaithful to me, O house of Israel, declares the Lord." -Jeremiah 3:20

What we need to take note of is that the real adultery in our homes may not involve another man or a woman. It may be spiritual infidelity. God is a jealous God. He does not take kindly to being two-timed. Just like sexual adultery will bring hell in the home, so will spiritual adultery.

As James indicates, too many of us in our homes have a friendship with the world. Friendship with the world means preferring the world's attractions, opinions, passions, goals, and pleasures. A checkpoint is needed here because being a friend to the world makes you an enemy of God.

James gets to the heart of the matter when he says: "But he gives us more grace. That is why Scripture says: God opposes the proud but gives grace to the humble." -James 4:6

There is grace available for your home.

- No matter what has been said – there is grace available.
- No matter what has been neglected – there is grace available.

- No matter how long it has been going on – there is grace available.

When you desire God's grace you need to humble yourself. To be humble means to have lowliness of mind. It is the opposite of being proud, which is to be conceited, puffed up, haughty or lifting yourself above another. Pride is something that can be hidden in the heart but it will ultimately come out in the open. The Word clearly says God "opposes" (meaning strongly resists like a military resistance) the proud.

When people are frustrated, angry or hurt they have to watch out for pride. "Pride goes before destruction, a haughty spirit before a fall." -Proverb 16:18

Your home can receive the benefits of God's grace if you go through the checkpoints. Humility will help turn your home around.

- It will position you to receive more grace.
- It will make your home privileged to have access to heaven's resources.
- It will cause you to be a peacemaker instead of a power broker.

One of the most ocular demonstrations of humility is going through a checkpoint. No matter how good you think you are, you still have to be searched. You have to get rid of some things that are not approved. You may have to take off some things. At the checkpoint you are under someone else's authority. At the checkpoint you may have something confiscated. At the checkpoint you may be denied entry. The checkpoint helps to maintain serenity, satisfaction and safety. Do not fly without a checkpoint!

Humble yourself and go through the spiritual checkpoint for your home. At the checkpoint you will find the Word of God, which contains the law and the Holy Spirit who enforces the law in our hearts.

NOTES

(L-R) Granddaughters, Layla and Elianah

*(L-R) Pastor Johnny Ogletree III with wife Quinita and daughters,
Adaiah, Layla and Elianah*

*(L-R) Sherrell, Quinita, Lambreni, Elianah, Layla, Adaiah, and
Reya*

INTRODUCTION

Our ministry is designed to strengthen the family. Therefore, throughout the year, God's truth for the family is proclaimed during our Sunday Services. In fact, we do Sermon Series dealing with the family, at least twice a year.

The following is a message on the family by Pastor O.

Photos (L-R) Jordan, Pastor Johnny, Pastor O, and Elder Joseph

Pastor O's mother, Marion Deckard

Pastor and Lady O Celebrating 23 Years in Ministry

"BACK TO BASICS"
LUKE 10:38-42

WE LIVE IN AN AMAZING AGE. We are living in bigger, better houses than our parents and fore-parents. We've matriculate further with degrees from outstanding academic universities. We're driving better, dressing better, and eating better.

We've got High Definition TV, Satellite Radio, Cable TV, Satellite TV, the internet, ipods, smart phones, emails, text messaging, Facebook, MySpace and Twitter. And we have the latest furniture and appliances. We've gotten into the hustle and bustle of living the life. We are busy, stressed out, always moving, upwardly mobile and constantly striving for something new.

Our kids our in TBall, Little League football, basketball and baseball, soccer YMCA programs, dance class, gymnastics, Tawkondo, music programs, school athletics, band, Boy Scouts, Girl Scouts... everything!

With all that we have going on, schedules, time-lines, goals, demands, needs, wants...a lot of pressure exists in our homes. Things are affecting our homes that damage our relationships and our relationship with God. Before we permanently damage or lose our homes, we need take a close look at our lifestyles and go back to the basics.

Back to Basics means a family's return to the essential things that are non-negotiable in the life of the family that please God and provide lasting strength and security.

In the story of Jesus' visit to the home of Martha there is a snapshot of the struggle in our homes. Martha, Mary and Lazarus lived in Bethany a small town near Jerusalem. As revealed in John chapter 11, they were close friends of Jesus and He visited their home often. This was a godly home that the Lord had no reservations visiting.

Luke records one such visit in chapter 10. When Jesus arrived, Martha welcomed him into the house. Her sister Mary took advantage of the visit and sat at Jesus' feet to be taught by the Lord. She was a woman but was accepted by Jesus which went against the grain of the cultural practice of that day. He encouraged women to study and know the Scriptures.

It was a privilege to have a Rabbi in one's home. It was even more of a privilege to have Jesus, the Son of God in the home. The two sisters approached Jesus' presence differently. Their behavior is instructive for us today.

To Martha's credit she had the gift of hospitality. She desired to meet the needs of her guest. She held back nothing. It is possible that Jesus arrived unexpectedly. If so, she did not complain about it or refuse to serve him. It is likely that he was accompanied by some or all of his disciples. Still, he was welcomed.

Reading between the lines, Mary had assisted Martha at first in the preparations for the special guest, but then she moved to the feet of Jesus to be taught. Martha then felt the pressure and burden of preparing all by herself.

She is a portrait of what's happening in our homes today. Luke says she *was distracted with much serving.* She was overwhelmed, anxious, troubled, cumbered, upset over, worried about…the preparations. The Message Bible reads: *Martha was pulled away by all she had to do in the kitchen.*

This is the state of many homes, people pulled away and distracted by all the issues, schedules, duties, goals, desires or needs. Our lives are complicated and burdened with the tyranny of the urgent. *What needs to be done next? I've got to do this! I've got to do that! Where are we heading? Why haven't we got it yet?*

This tyranny:

- Tears one apart inwardly
- Triggers tension in relationships
- Turns attention away from the very things needed for triumphal living.

Martha left the kitchen went to the Lord and registered her complaint. *Lord, do you not care that my sister has left me to serve alone?* No doubt she was thinking: *Excuse me Lord, but I'm cooking all by my self? My sister should be helping me, not sitting here with You. I don't mind serving you but I need some help. Tell her then to help me!*

But the Lord responded without any affirmation of her stress. Notice His response: *Martha, Martha, you are anxious and troubled about many things, but one thing is necessary. Mary has chosen the good portion, which will not be taken from her.* In so many words, Jesus tells her: *Calm down, you need to go back to basics.* What Jesus gets her and us to see is the difference between what is negotiable and what is a non-negotiable. Busy stuff is negotiable, being fed spiritually is a non-negotiable. Ask yourself: *Is my home out of balance?* If yes, you need to go back to the basics.

Martha had become preoccupied with preparing the food while Mary was preoccupied with getting spiritually fed. Mary was focused on the basics, what would feed her soul. She wanted the meal that Jesus fixed. She wanted what was essential, what was indispensable to her life, what was fundamental to being a disciple of Jesus. That's the attitude and action that we need in our families.

We are too preoccupied with the temporary. We are too preoccupied with the non-essentials. We are too preoccupied with what will not add value, love, peace, joy, unity… We are working on this and on that but missing the good portion. The good portion is guaranteed to bring a return. The good portion is graded high by heaven. The good portion is what you can look back on and be grateful for.

We are going to suggest to you four areas for you to choose like Mary that are basic to your family's being in good hands.

1. The First Basic: Faith

Martha forgot how important faith in Jesus was to her life. She was too busy, too stress, too trouble about many things.

We have gotten so preoccupied with fortune and finances that we neglect the essential of faith in our families. We need to get back to having family prayer, living by Biblical principles, going to church giving your time, talent and your treasure to God's kingdom, sitting at the feet of Jesus and seeking God's face and favor for our homes. The basic understanding in our homes must be what it was for the children of Israel:

> *Hear, O Israel: The LORD our God, the LORD is one.*
> *You shall love the Lord your God with all your heart and*
> *with all your soul and with all your might. And these*
> *word that I command you today shall be on your heart.*
> *You shall teach them diligently to your children, and shall*
> *talk of them when you sit in your house, and when you*
> *walk by the way, and when you lie down, and when you*
> *rise. Deuteronomy 6:4-7 (ESV)*

Today, we have gotten so caught up in the pursuit of things that:

- we sacrifice our desire for family
- we sacrifice our marriages
- we sacrifice our children, God must be first!

We fail to realize what Jesus says is true about the titles, positions, homes, cars, clothes, jewelry and money—it can all be taken away.

All things will fade away. We need to have a God-centered home for nothing can separate us from the love of God. Somebody needs to get back to basics and draw a line and say what Joshua said:

> …*choose this day whom you will serve… But as for me and my house, we will serve the LORD. Joshua 24:15*

Get back to basics!

2. The Second Basic for the home is working Together.

We have gotten so busy in our family dynamic that we have lost the art of working together. Jesus stresses this basic principle when He said: **And if a house is divided against itself, that house will not be able to stand. (Mark 3:25)**

The home is the basic unit of cooperation in society. It is where the understanding should develop that you need family to succeed. The home is where one should eliminate the spirit of selfishness and cultivate an appreciation for the complimenting one another.

Working together is very important for fulfillment in a family. The enemy wants to divide and cause confusion, hurt, disappointment and tension. Martha thought that Mary wasn't doing her part so she complained. When there is a belief that someone is not doing their part negative feelings will result.

Areas to work together:

- Income (everyone works)
- Raising children
- Household chores
- Special seasons (sickness, school)

What Paul wrote in Philippians will work in the home: *be of the same mine, having the same love, being in full accord and of one mine.*

Do nothing from rivalry or conceit, but in humility count others more significant than yourselves. Philippians 2:2, 3

Get back to basics!

3. The Third basic is Demonstrating Love.

It may seem silly but one of the basics we need to emphasize is the demonstration of love one to another. Loving the way God desires is action   not a feeling or a thought. Love should be expressed and demonstrated.

Listen to the Word on this issue:

> *Greater love has no one than this that someone lay down his life for his friends. John 15:13 Love is patient and kind; loves does not envy or boast; it is not arrogant or rude. It does not insist on its way, it is not irritable or resentful; it does not rejoice at wrongdoing, but rejoices with truth. Loves bears all thing, believes all things, hopes all things, endures all things. 1 Corinthians 13:4-7*

The demonstration of love includes, hugs, kisses, words of encouragement, forgiveness, cards, flowers, gifts, dinners…   Both Martha and Mary had to demonstrate their love for each other after the tension that day when Jesus visited. There will be misunderstandings, arguments, hurt feelings and anger in a home from time to time but the Word says this about love: ***love covers a multitude of sins. (1 Peter 4:8)*** The Message Bible reads: ***Love makes up for practically anything.***

Since we live with imperfect people, we need something to make up for each other's sins, short-comings and faults. The only thing that will work is love. Martha had a fault of worrying, complaining and becoming to preoccupied with stuff. Still Mary had the responsibility of letting love cover her hurt and anger. The word cover means to hide or conceal therefore the demonstration of love acts as if the harm hasn't occurred.

That's the type of love that Jesus had to cover our sins.

4. **The Forth Basic is Rest and Relaxation.**

A sure cure for a busy, stressed out life is rest and relaxation. This needs to be a non-negotiable for everyone. We are working and worrying ourselves to death—literally. Jesus is our example for this:

> **And Levi made him a great feast in his house, and there was a large company of tax collectors and others reclining at table with them. Luke 5:29**
>
> **Jesus withdrew with his disciples to the sea... Mark 3:7**

Jesus was not all work and no play. He rested and relaxed. He loved to be in the company of his disciples without the crowd. The same needs to take place within our families. We need times of rest together. We need times of relaxation together. We need to refresh ourselves, renew ourselves and revive ourselves.

We need vacations, weekend get-a ways, private moments together. We need to take advantage of holidays and spend quality time together establishing precious memories for our families.

What this message is about is how we can return to the essential things, the non-negotiable things that please God and provide lasting strength and security for the family. When we go back to the basics we stand a greater chance to be:

- The best parents we can be
- The best husbands and wives

- The best sons and daughters
- The best grandparents
- The best aunties and uncles
- The best friends

What is important for our homes is to have God in the lives of each family member and remember we need God, not the stuff, not the money, not the schedule. Let get **"Back to Basics."**

"NO LIMITS" LIVING FOR THE FAMILY"

This is the Year of No Limits at First Met. We believe that God wants our ministry, our families and our individual members to experience the exceedingly abundantly above all that could be asked for or thought mentioned in Ephesians 3:20.

- God desires this for your singleness.
- God desires this for your marriage.
- God desires this for your children.
- God desires this for your finances.
- God desires this for your health.

We know that many of you do not experience this in your lives. You live with and face limits daily, weekly, and monthly. In our many years of counseling, we constantly see one impediment to experiencing "no limits" in the homes of God's people—Baggage.

Baggage is defined as those things that encumber one's freedom, progress, development or adaptability. It is superfluous or burdensome practices or ideas.

Every individual single or married has "baggage" or previous experiences in life that get in the way of experiencing the abundant living of God. Everyone possesses or acquires baggage during their upbringing or relationships.

- Parental neglect, abuse or negligence—"Baggage."
- Prior relationship wounds or hurts—"Baggage."
- Past failures in school or employment—"Baggage."
- Perverted indulgencies or practices—"Baggage."
- Patterns of perceived persecution—"Baggage."

- Pushed aside having not been popular—"Baggage."
- Popular to the point of excess pride—"Baggage."

How do you know if you have baggage?

Baggage loads a person's mind with negativity, doubt, revenge, jealousy, envy, discord, paranoia, and low self-esteem… It promotes or encourages or causes anger, depression, meanness, sickness, selfishness, grief, conflict, fleshly endeavors, self-defeating behavior or sin.

How do you identify your baggage?

There are different types of baggage for travel that parallel emotional, mental or spiritual baggage:

- Carry On—light, full of personal items you want to keep close and you don't want out of your sight.
- Garment Bag—holds the expensive things that remind you of special occasions.
- Overnight Bag—carries for small things for a brief stay.
- Suitcase—holds many diverse things and good for stuffing the things.
- Trunk—this is for old stuff that you just can't let go of, like memories, nostalgia good and bad.

When traveling by air there are limitations on the amount, size and weight of baggage one can take on airplane trip. Each airline has a **Baggage Allowance, which** allows a passenger to check a maximum number (2) at a certain size and weight limit (no more than 50 lbs.).

We need a **Baggage Allowance** for believers to prevent the emotional, mental and spiritual damage that blinds and binds peace, joy, happiness, prosperity, romance, the nurture of children, and spiritual growth. Singles, before you get married you need a Baggage Allowance. Couples, you need a Baggage Allowance. Whenever you attempt to take more baggage (in number or weight) on a plane you have to pay an additional charge.

When you exceed the allowance, you have what is known as **Excess Baggage.** Excess means more that what is allowed. Many a person is hindered by excess baggage. Many a marriage is held back by excess baggage. Many a child is hampered by excess baggage.

Airlines charge for Excess Baggage. You must understand that each airplane has a maximum capacity weight limit for it to fly safely. And, so it is with the family, there is a maximum weight limit to live safely and reach a God given destiny. The more baggage you have the more it costs you as an individual and as a family. It costs sleep, money, time, joy and blessings from heaven.

What to do with excess baggage:

The writer of Hebrews writes in chapter 12 verse 1:

> *"Therefore, we also, since we are surrounded by so great a crowd of witnesses, let us lay aside every weight, and the sin which so easily ensnares us, and let us run with endurance the race that is set before us, looking to Jesus, the author and finisher of our faith, who for the joy that was set before Him endured the cross, despising the shame, and has sat down at the right hand of the throne of God.*
> *(NKJV)*

The writer teaches that races are to be run with maximum weight for minimum restrictions. A runner needs a certain pace and endurance for a race. One of the major obstacles to a runner's ability is excess weight. The word used in the text means an encumbrance that will handicap. What is there in your life encumbers or handicaps your life or your family?

The writer says that a race can be hindered by sin that is easily entangles or ensnares. This is sin that is specifically enticing to you or your situation. It is the sin that is just standing around waiting on you to succumb to it so that it can hinder you, your marriage or your family.

Therefore the writer says: "lay aside every weight and the sin." This means t*o get rid of, to put aside or cast off.* The writer knows that there are things that taint or tarnish, degrade or dishonor a believer. So the writer puts the responsibility on the individual not on God or another person to get rid of the problem. It is the responsibility of the believer to get him or her clean. It is not your mother or father's responsibility, not your "boo's" responsibility, not your husband or wife or child's responsibility. If you have Excess Baggage, it's your responsibility to get rid of it.

- Pray your baggage away.
- Praise your baggage away.
- Confess your baggage away.
- Study your baggage away.
- Fellowship your baggage away.
- Sow your baggage away.
- Believe your baggage away.
- Practice your baggage away.

When traveling, excess can be handled by getting rid of a piece of luggage or taking something out of a piece of luggage. Someone for the sake of your home needs to get rid of a piece of luggage. Get rid of unnecessary baggage one piece at a time.

Someone else may need to take something out of what you've packed. Look again at what you don't need. The weight, you don't need. The burden, you don't need. The stress, you don't need. The anger, you don't need. The frustration, you don't need. Remove something you packed!

And still there are others who've been traveling life's journey whether as a single person, married or parent headed to a new destination. You've got your baggage checked it is not excessive but it is still baggage. Here's a suggestion for you: Leave the **baggage unclaimed!**

- Don't pick it up again.
- Don't weigh yourself down again.
- Don't pull it or push it again.

Each load in your bag keeps you from getting better especially when you mix old stuff with the new. You can't get needed items in your bag when you have plenty of old unnecessary stuff. The tendency is to get comfortable with the way things are even if they are bad or unnecessary.

The airlines have an elaborate baggage handling system to identify and deliver luggage to each traveler. The enemy also has a baggage handling system to make sure your baggage travels with you. He wants your baggage to show up wherever you are. Baggage will show up at the dinner table, bedroom, in the car, or at the church.

Free yourself, your marriage, your children, and your family for a "No Limits" experience with God.

- No limits in communication
- No limits in understanding
- No limits in peace
- No limits in romance
- No limits in finances
- No limits in dreams and hopes

The writer says run and run with endurance or patience. It means to run even when you encounter troubles and trials. It means run without doubt or despair. And while you are running, look to Jesus the author and finisher of our faith. Jesus has paid the price for you to have a No Limits experience in your homes so get rid of your baggage.

ABOUT THE AUTHOR

We are now blessed to have four children (three sons and one daughter). All are married except our youngest son, Jordan. Our first son is our Youth Pastor, is married to Quinita and has four gorgeous daughters. Our second child Lambreni is married to Avery and has two daughters and one son. Our third child, Joe is married to Sherrill and they have one son and expecting their second son in a few months. All of our children and spouses are college graduates and come from good homes. They all love the Lord and work in ministry. They are raising their children to love the Lord as they were raised. We had to fight for our home and helping them to fight to keep Satan out of their homes. We don't take sides, they are always on the Lord's side ready to give the word when there are problems. Our motto is "A Family that Prays Together, Plays Together, and Pulls Together will always be Together". We make memories and get together weekly. When we are together having fun, watching our grandchildren, we know that our laboring together, on fighting Satan together was not in vain.

John D. Ogletree, Jr. is a native of Dallas, Texas. He obtained a Bachelors degree from the University of Texas at Arlington in 1973 and a Doctor of Jurisprudence degree from South Texas College of Law in Houston, Texas in 1979. He accepted the call into the gospel ministry in 1982. In 1985, he was ordained at Antioch Missionary Baptist Church. He became the founding pastor of *First Metropolitan Baptist Church in 1986.* Pastor Ogletree provided leadership in the purchase of 25.2 acres of land along Beltway 8 in Northwest Houston. He is a Trustee on the CyFair-Independent School District Board. Pastor Ogletree served as Chair and Vice-Chair of the Executive Board of the Baptist General Convention of Texas. He serves as President of African American Fellowship Association in the Baptist General Convention of Texas. He is past Moderator of the Union Baptist Association. He holds a myriad of workshops including these topics: ABCs of Leadership Excellence, Building Team Capacity, Empowering Leaders, Leading for High Performance, Leaders Setting the Pace, Unlocking the Doors of Faith, Moving to the Next Level (*a must for today's church leaders*), Leadership During a Crisis, and Marriage and the Family. Pastor Ogletree is the author of *Moving to the Next Level* (*Becoming a Fully Developing Follower of Christ*). Pastor Ogletree has been married to his wife Evelyn for 35 years. They are the parents of three sons: Johnny, Joseph, and Jordan; and one daughter, Lambreni. They have six granddaughters (Layla, Elianah, Adaiah, Nessiah, Reya, and Elan) and two grandsons (Zion and Jaiden). He can be reached at PastorO@firstmet.org.

Evelyn Ogletree, First Lady of First Metropolitan Church (Houston, TX,), affectionately known as Lady O, was born in Tyler, Texas but grew up in Dallas. She has always had a close relationship with the Lord and has a special anointing that is revealed through her personal life and in her ministry with her husband. She is currently pursuing her doctorate degree at Texas A&M University in Urban Education. Lady O is a former schoolteacher for HISD, KISD and Cy-Fair ISD. She is Director of the Infant Development Center (IDC) and Christian Academy that provides guidance and day care for children ages 6 weeks to five years of age, as well as an after-school program for grade school children that is open to the community. In 1999, Lady O was called to the ministry. She currently serves as Executive Pastor and Executive Director of Redemption Community Development Corporation. Lady O preaches and teaches the Word of God, as well as, speaks at conferences on subjects such as Marriage and the Family, Child Rearing, and does consultations for Ministers' and Pastors' wives. Her joy in life is spent speaking to all issues confronting today's women. Each year she leads the women at First Met in their Annual Women's Conference, "*Daughters at the Feet of Jesus*". For information on the conference, please contact her at LadyO@ firstmet.org

In an exclusive interview with Pastor Ogletree, affectionately known as "Pastor O" by his congregation, the author and international speaker shared his journey to prominence. He had a vision of a church that would truly make disciples for Christ and would be a place to raise children – a place where families could grow together. As author of the popular book, *Moving to the Next Level*, he is drawing major attention across the country. Ogletree says he is pleased that the book did well. Pastors of large and small churches are still using his book for leadership workshops.

He said these are serious times because "churches are competing with a very secularized, permissive, demonic, capitalistic, and materialistic culture." According to Ogletree, "People have many options and most of them are subtle and subliminal. People don't realize how powerfully they are being impacted by ungodly influences. In addition, people are in an age where everything is relative and people don't want to believe in absolute truths". To him, this is a real challenge for the church, today - a challenge that he is willing to fight.

When asked how they manage their many roles, they said learning to bring balance into their life was the key. He chuckled, "when we first started out, I thought it was the church first, but of course, Lady O let me know that was not going to work. I could not put the church and the people of the church before her and my family. I had to change. I know it is God first, my family and then the church." This meant spending "intentional time" with his wife and children. He said his wife is a partner in the ministry and plays a significant role in the church. They pray together, talk about the direction of the church and everything else from budgets, to leadership, to sermon series, to "ups and downs." He emphasized her influence in his decision-making and sees her as "invaluable."

As people see First Met as they travel the Beltway, it is a spiritual magnet in the community. First Met has become a "major spiritual force" on the Beltway.